Welcoming

the Nations Among Us

✦

**Engage with your cross-cultural
neighbors for the sake of the gospel**

ISBN: 978-1-947468-93-1

Published by Via Nations
PO Box 3556
Fayetteville, AR 72702
For more resources, visit vianations.org

Translations
We desire to make this material available to as many as will use it around the world
in a way that honors everyone involved in the work. If you would like to translate or
adapt this resource to use in your cultural context, we are very open to collaborating
with you. There are guidelines for translators at vianations.org/translation.

Printed in Canada through Bookmark

Second Edition, First Imprint, 2023
C 10-5-22   M 3-1-23 14:15

Contents

Introduction

Today is an exciting time in history to be a part of God's mission. In the 21st century of globalization and migration, welcoming is becoming a key strategy for the global church to obey Christ's command to go make disciples of all nations.

WHAT IS WELCOMING?

Welcoming is more than being friendly. It is the lifestyle of a person prioritizing God's mission to "make disciples of all nations." A welcomer gets involved with those around them from different cultures. This may be in their neighborhood, city, or region. Welcoming means developing genuine cross-cultural friendships, selflessly serving, and always being ready to share Jesus with others.

The foundation of welcoming finds its basis in the biblical theme of God's mission to redeem all peoples. It is about his compassion for all peoples especially the outsider. The term "welcoming" is not used in the Bible, but the concept is taught and practiced throughout Scripture.

WHY WELCOME?

The global church has never been larger, more geographically spread out, or more ethnically diverse. Today, because of migration, the vast majority of the global evangelical church is living in close proximity to peoples who have never heard the gospel.

Read that last paragraph again. No longer must a Christian travel to another country or learn another language to interact with the unreached — the unreached have come to us! God is using migration to bring lost people into relationship with himself. Every Christian can get excited about that. Regardless of your political views on migration or what is happening in your

> **ⓘ Unreached people group**
>
> a group that has no access to the good news of Jesus because his people are too few to see an ongoing movement of churches planted

country with immigrants, Jesus wants you to see them as people he loves and died for—people worthy of your time, of your compassion, and of hearing the good news about him.

THE PURPOSE OF THIS STUDY

God invites us to explore welcoming others for his glory. He has a role for you. Our Father has always been a welcomer and has a role for you to play in joining him. Come explore the realities of migrants and near neighbors around you, your own obstacles to reaching out cross-culturally, and how you can take practical steps to start welcoming.

SENSITIVE CONTENT

A warning: there are a few stories in this booklet that can be difficult to read. It may be painful to imagine the experiences that these men, women, and children have lived, but we believe facing the reality of their situations is key to welcoming them well.

THE WORLD CHRISTIAN SERIES

This study is part of the World Christian Series. World Christians are people who understand God's heart for the world and strategically live their lives in such a way that wherever they are and whatever they do, they are working to see him glorified among all nations. Daily practices, such as praying, can be expanded into practical World Christian Habits that we as Christians can implement in order to reach God's heart for other communities across the world. *Explore the World Christian Lifestyle* introduces the five Habits, and other studies in the World Christian Series dive deeper into each particular habit. These include:

01 Praying
02 Sending
03 Welcoming
04 Going
05 Mobilizing

Lesson 01

The Biblical Basis *of* Welcoming

> For the Lord will have compassion on Jacob and will again choose Israel, and will set them in their own land, and sojourners will join them and will attach themselves to the house of Jacob.
>
> —Isaiah 14:1

✳ Prep

01   When you hear the words "refugee" or "foreigner," what comes to mind? Share a few honest reactions.

02   Were the people who came to your mind from a particular religion? Ethnicity? Poor or wealthy? Educated or not? Dangerous? Old or young? What language did they speak?

03   How did you arrive at this image?

It is easy for us to have mistaken beliefs and prejudice toward foreigners. Throughout history, people have always done this, but God never has. God loves all ethnicities and is eager to bring them his love and salvation. "God loved the whole world" (John 3:16) and sent Jesus to die so he could save people from "every tribe, language, people, and nation" (Rev 5:9).

As more and more people around the world are on the move, governments are increasingly thinking about and even dividing over migration issues. Does God speak about the foreigner who has come to your community and how we should treat them? God is not silent about the cause of the refugee, the immigrant, or the outsider. In fact, our God is a God who identifies with and

enters into their distress. People moving to new lands is as old as Genesis, and God has often used and directed migration for his own purposes. In fact, welcoming has always been a significant part of God's mission to reach all peoples. In this study we explore how welcoming is rooted in the Law, expressed by faithful Israel, modeled by Jesus, and practiced by the church.

" Discuss

God Establishes a Welcomer Nation

In Genesis 12:1-3, God calls Abram to begin a great nation and to be a foreigner in a new land. Isaac, Jacob, and their descendants were immigrants, refugees, and slaves. In Exodus, God uses another refugee and foreigner, Moses, to deliver Israel from Egypt.

After the exodus, Israel became a people without a nation, wandering in foreign lands for forty years. There were many others who played a central

role in God's story of salvation. Some were part of God's people but lived as foreigners (Joseph, Daniel, Nehemiah, Jonah), while others were Gentiles (non-Jews) who became part of God's people (Rahab, Ruth).

Foreigners are often seen as outsiders, treated unjustly, and taken advantage of. In contrast to the way most people treated foreigners, God expressly commanded his people to act differently toward the foreigner. From the very beginning, Israel was called to be a "welcomer nation."

ℹ Welcoming

initiating a relationship with and being a witness for Christ to those from a different culture or ethnicity who are living nearby

Jesus Models Welcoming

There were many ethnicities living among the Jews who were treated poorly because they were not part of "God's chosen people." Yet thousands came to Jesus, many of them needing help. Jesus welcomed them all, traveled to them, ate with them, healed them, proclaimed the kingdom to them, and loved them.

01   **Read Luke 10:25–37.**

Here Jesus teaches what it looks like to both love God *and* love our neighbor by making the hero a member of a despised ethnic group—the Samaritans—instead of an honored priest or Levite. What is Jesus saying about the outsider in this story? What response do you think he is looking for from his followers?

02 **Read Matthew 25:34–43.**

Here Jesus is judging the nations and uses some startling criteria. What does this say about those on the outside of society? What response might Jesus be looking for from those who heard this? (Bonus: How could our treatment of outsiders be a basis for judgment versus faith in him?)

Digging Deeper
For further study and a more complete list of foreigners in the Bible, see the Appendix: Lesson 1.

Foreigners and Citizens

03 **Read Philippians 3:20; Ephesians 2:11–13,19; and Hebrews 11:13,16.**

To what lengths did Jesus go to welcome us when we were foreigners to God? As Christians, how are we both citizens and foreigners? How might this shape our perspective, identity, and treatment of others?

Summary

04   God is on a global mission to bring salvation to all ethnic groups. God designed his chosen people to be a welcomer nation because he is a welcomer God. Jesus embraced outsiders and modeled welcoming to his disciples. The early church became foreigners for the sake of the gospel as they moved out from Jerusalem, seeing themselves as citizens of a heaven (Book of Acts). What might change if the global church actively welcomed foreigners?

❧ Live

Make It Personal

01   What does it say about the God of the Bible that he is concerned about the foreigner? What does it say that so much of his redemptive work has been carried out by "foreigners?"

02   Are you convinced from the Bible that our God is someone who enters into the distress of the foreigner and calls his people to welcome them? Why or why not? What questions remain?

03   How do God's attitudes and actions of "welcoming the foreigner" contrast with the views of your society or even your church?

Make it Real

04   Write a Personal Welcome Statement or summary of what God has taught you about himself, his people, and foreigners. Share what God taught you with one other person this week.

05   How has God's Word renewed your mind or convicted your heart of a new truth regarding foreigners? How do you think you need to change? Share a way and pray for one another.

_____

_____

_____

_____

Digging Deeper

Read Luke 7:1–10. Here Jesus welcomes the enemy—a captain of a foreign military who was currently occupying Israel. What is Jesus saying about the outsider in this story? What response do you think he is looking for from his followers? Why might these verses be important to the idea of welcoming?

See the Appendix: Lesson 1 for more on the Biblical Basis of Welcoming.

Lesson 02

The Need *and the* Opportunity

" For there will never cease to be poor in the land. Therefore I command you, 'You shall open wide your hand to your brother, to the needy and to poor, in your land.'

—Deuteronomy 15:11

✳ Prep

In the first lesson, we explored God as a welcomer of all people made in his image. Throughout the Bible, he also calls his people to be models of his love and justice, especially by welcoming those who are overlooked by society or seen as foreigners.

God desires the whole gospel to go out from the whole church to the whole world. But what if God has sovereignly brought the whole world to us? Massive migrations are occurring all over the world, usually moving people to places where they can have much greater access to the gospel. In our lifetime alone, millions of people have come within reach of God's people for the first time. They are looking for help, belonging, and a better life. Many are open to or actively seeking Jesus.

01   How do you see this as an opportunity? How do you see this as a threat?

Migration and God's Design

We see in the Bible that God has used migration in the past to help people discover him. God is doing the same thing today. Carefully read this excerpt from Paul preaching in Athens:

> ❶ **Migration**
>
> the voluntary or involuntary movement of people from one location to another

> "From one man he made all the nations, that they should inhabit the whole earth; and he marked out their appointed times in history and the boundaries of their lands. God did this so that they would seek him and perhaps reach out for him and find him, though he is not far from any one of us." (Acts 17:26-27)

Today, the Holy Spirit is inspiring more and more Christians like us to become personally involved in welcoming foreigners. Of the 600 million Bible-believing Christians in the world, 80% live in Africa, Asia, and Latin America.[1] The church has never been larger, more ethnically diverse, or more geographically spread out. Followers of Jesus can impact formerly unreached peoples like never before because they are coming to us.

" Discuss

Migration Realities

- The world population almost tripled from 2.5 billion to 7 billion from 1950 to 2010.[2]

- In 1800, 3% of people lived in cities. In 2007 more than half the world lived in cities. By 2050 almost 70% of the world's population will live in cities.[3]

- In 1900, London was the largest city in the world with 5 million people. In 1950 there were two cities with 10 million people. By 2030 projections estimate there will be 43 mega-cities of over 10 million people each. Tokyo alone is 38 million people.[4]

- If current trends continue, by 2050, 40% of all Africans will live in slums (840 million) as well as 23% of the global population (2 billion).[5]

- The Jesus Film (an evangelistic movie of the life of Jesus) is available in over 1600 languages on any smartphone, crossing borders and following migrants.[6]

- In 2000, Muslims comprised 3% of the population of Europe. With current trends of birth rate and immigration, Islam is projected to be 17% in 2050.

Many of these people will be from highly restricted countries hostile to the gospel.[7]

- 245 million (roughly 1 out of 9) Christians globally experience a high level of persecution for their faith. In Asia, it is 1 out of 3. Persecution is one of the top reasons for migration.[8]

- 40 million people today are victims of slavery. This is more than at any other time in history.[9]

- Population projections through 2050 predict additions of 100 million new immigrants to North America and 50 million to Europe. Additionally, they

> "
> Countries with the highest population growth are also the ones least able to deal with more growth. This is due to inadequate goveranance, education, and infrastructure as well as instability in society. The result is higher livels of vrime, diease, and poverty. This will lead to greater levels of migration in the future. —PATRICK JOHNSTONE, Global Population expert

predict population decreases of 40 million from South America, 34 million from Africa, and 27 million from Central Asia.[10]

- Over 22% of the world's population is ethnically Chinese. Fifty million of these live outside China. For example, about 7 million Chinese live in Indonesia, and 43% are Christians.[11]

- English and Mandarin are the most spoken languages in the world with 1.1 billion speakers followed by Hindi (615 million), and Spanish (534 million).[12]

- Sex trafficking is a $99 billion a year industry. Twenty-one million adults and children are bought and sold worldwide into commercial sexual servitude, forced labor and bonded labor. Women and girls make up 96% of victims.[13]

01   Reflect on these statistics. What impacts you and why?

The Stories Behind Migration

Read through these stories of real people, real difficulties, and real hope. Let them invite you into the realities of their lives and situations. *(Names and locations have been changed for protection.)*

Hadi and Maryam: We lived in a Muslim country where Christian persecution is common. When the government increased its persecution of Christians in my town, we decided to leave. We traveled with our one-year-old son for over a year from Iraq to France via North Africa. We walked most of the way, trying to find friends to stay with and working to save up enough money for the next part of the journey. We were smuggled across borders on foot, by boat, bus, and truck. Somehow, we made it to France, but upon arrival we became victims of Sharia law in the refugee camp because my wife did not dress modestly enough. We were labeled troublemakers by the authorities, endangering our request for asylum. My wife broke down. The authorities threatened to take away our son because she was not fit, making the problem worse. We were sent to live in a tiny French-speaking town of 300 people. We know almost no French. We have no friends, no church, no community. We spend most days never leaving our flat. Yesterday we were notified our son received a place in a school in a nearby city. We are praying they will send us there so we do not have to travel 45 minutes each way by bus.

Rashid: I am Emirati, but grew up in several countries as my dad moved around for work as a banker. I have lived in four countries and speak three languages. My family is very influential in the UAE, and much is expected of me. I have been accepted into the finance program at the University of London. This is my first week on campus. Today I met Tony, a Christian student from Australia who invited me to a worship night with his friends. I am planning to go.

Ibrahim: I was an imam from a respected family in Libya. I was sent to Greece from my homeland to plant mosques. One night, however, I met Jesus in a dream. I then met some Christians and started to follow him. When I went back home to see my wife and family, they nearly beat me to death and gave my wife to another man. God preserved my life. I moved to Sweden to share Christ with the people who had come there from my country. One day, I was found out by local Muslims, beaten, and stabbed twice. It took me many months to recover. Today I still share Jesus around the country and have helped plant hundreds of house churches across Sweden among North Africans. I also met a wonderful Swedish woman who loves Jesus. We married earlier this year.

Nestle: I am a 16-year-old from Syria. I found myself alone in the world after seeing my whole family die in a missile attack on my village. Everything was burned to the ground. I fled with my brother, the only one who escaped the village alive, but he was killed in front of me when he stepped on a land mine. Now I am alone in a camp for orphaned children in Turkey. I have not felt safe since that day. I have nowhere to go and no prospects for the future. I often attract the advances of men in the neighboring camp. Last night I was raped and beaten.

Li Jie: I grew up in Shanghai. I went to university in the West and graduated with a double major in politics and economics. I returned to China where a good position in the government awaited me. However, since my time back I have been conflicted. I follow Jesus now and have experienced freedoms

I had never known. I want others to be free from sin, free from oppression, free to follow Jesus. My heart breaks for my people.

✦

02   Reflect on these stories of real people. What impacts you?

Walk in the Shoes of a Foreigner

Have someone read aloud the excerpt of a poem below. Close your eyes and listen. Imagine yourself in this situation. Immerse yourself in the scene, the tastes, touches, smells, sights, and noises. What if this were your family? Can you feel the loss, the fear, the isolation, and the indignity? What could experiencing God's love mean for one of these people?

No one leaves home unless home is the mouth of a shark
You only run for the border when you see the whole city running as well

Your neighbors running faster than you
You have to understand that no one puts their children in a boat
Unless the water is safer than the land
No one burns their palms under trains
No one spends days and nights in the stomach of a truck
Feeding on newspaper unless the miles traveled means something more
   than the journey
No one crawls under fences
No one wants to be beaten
Pitied

No one chooses refugee camps
Go home blacks
Refugees
Dirty immigrants
Asylum seekers
Sucking our country dry
They smell strange
Savage
They messed up their country and now they want to mess up ours
How do the words, the dirty looks, roll off your backs?

Maybe because the blow is softer or the insults are easier to swallow
Than rubble, than bone, than your child's body in pieces.
I want to go home, but home is the mouth of a shark
Home is the barrel of the gun
Leave your clothes behind, crawl through the desert, wade through the oceans
Drown, save, be hungry, beg, forget pride
Your survival is more important

No one leaves home until home is a sweaty voice in your ear
Saying—
Leave, run away from me now
I don't know what I've become
But I know that anywhere is safer than here

—EXCERPT FROM "HOME," BY WARSAN SHIRE, A BRITISH-SOMALI POET

03   Reflect on this perspective. What are you feeling and thinking?

_____

_____

_____

_____

Instead of hardening our hearts like the rest of the world and pretending
this does not affect us, let us do something to change it. Perhaps loving our
neighbor with the love of Jesus would not only bring healing to those who are
forced to move, but could also bring healing to our own souls, and maybe to
our society.

As migration increases, how can we as Christians rise to the challenge,
enter into the lives of the foreigners who surround us, and develop new
multicultural communities of faith that truly reflect God's heart for all peoples
(Revelation 7:9)? This may be the biggest challenge facing the church in the
next 50 years.

The world is at your door. There are too many opportunities to love our
neighbor to ever be bored as a Christian. Open the door. Walk across the
street. Open your life. Bring them to the only one who can heal, redeem, and
offer them an eternal place to belong and a family they can never lose.

✿ Live

Make it Personal

01   In your own words, explain why welcoming foreigners could be important for you as a Christian. (Matthew 11:28-30, 22:37, 28:19-20 may provide insights.)

02   How would I want to be treated if I had to leave my home, my family, my community, my country? Be detailed and descriptive.

04 Where could you go this week to meet a new person from a different
culture? Who could go with you?

05 Read the poem to someone this week and share with them something
you learned from this chapter. (Share what happens with your group
next week.)

Lesson 03

Who Can I Welcome?

> He executes justice for the fatherless and the widow, and loves the sojourner, giving him food and clothing. Love the sojourner, therefore, for you were sojourners in the land of Egypt.
>
> —Deuteronomy 10:18-19

✳ Prep

Lift Up Your Eyes

We see people around us every day, but rarely stop to truly look at them. Have you ever looked at a person on the street, on a bus, at a restaurant and wondered about their life, their struggles, their dreams? As humans, we treat people differently based on superficial qualities. We naturally make distinctions. Many times it is based on assumptions or misinformation we receive from our culture. But how does God view people?

> ❝
> Look beneath the surface so you can judge correctly.
> —JESUS (JOHN 7:24)

God's Perspective

There is a familiar story — a welcoming story — where Jesus taught God's disciples to see people from God's perspective.

01 **Read John 4:7-9, 19-42.**

Here we have four scenes: Jesus crossing cultures, sharing the good news, teaching the disciples a lesson, and the result of one believer on a community. "I tell you, open your eyes and look at the fields! They are ripe for harvest."

Who is the ripe harvest Jesus was referring to? Why could the disciples not see it? What does this have to do with welcoming foreigners?

We too must hear Jesus' challenging words to "open your eyes" to the spiritual harvest near us. Let's look at the different types of people who are on the move so that we might understand their needs, step into the harvest around us, and welcome them like Jesus.

" Discuss

Open Your Eyes to See Immigrants

Immigrants are those who leave their own country willingly and most often with the intent of living permanently in a new country. We are including migrant workers in this category too, even though most migrant workers are in foreign countries for a limited length of time and often return home. Both immigrants and migrant workers are often low-skilled, hardworking laborers who want better pay. They are pulled by the offer of a better life. 232 million people globally fit into this category.

MEET A BIBLICAL IMMIGRANT

I was doing this for my family. My mother-in-law was the only family I had left after my husband died, and I would do anything to take care of her. So, I came to this new land as a permanent immigrant. It was a scary time because this wasn't my home or my culture, and I often felt fearful, vulnerable, and alone. But luckily, the good people of this land provide opportunities for the poor and foreigners to live, work, and meet their needs. I went out every day and worked hard to support the two of us. My boss was so kind and welcoming. He made sure my basic needs were provided for. Then a miracle happened; the man not only provided me with a job, he also married me! He looked past my poverty, the social stigmas, and all the cultural barriers to see my integrity, to see who I really was. Now

I live as part of God's people. I hope to pass on the value of welcoming outsiders to my children, grandchildren, and great-grandchildren.
—RUTH, A MOABITE, DIRECT ANCESTOR OF JESUS

NEEDS OF IMMIGRANTS

By nature, immigrants often come from difficult situations that have compelled them to move in order to find a better life for their families. Immigrants will feel out of place in their new culture, and can be hard to reach because they often remain within insular ethnic communities or move frequently following job opportunities. Technology has improved their immigration experience, allowing them to connect with family and find useful information, yet many remain very isolated from friends and family. Things like language learning, access to healthcare, knowing and meeting legal immigration requirements, finding community, and dealing with stress associated with cross-cultural transition are all normal needs most immigrants have.

REFLECTING ON IMMIGRANTS

01   It is a difficult decision for anyone who chooses to leave their home, family, culture, and everything familiar to find better opportunities. What might cause you to leave your family, culture and country? What might it cost you?

Open Your Eyes to See Refugees

A refugee is a person who has been forced to leave their home country in order to escape war, persecution, or natural disaster. These people are unable to return to their home country given the current situation. They are fully dependent on their host country to provide safety and the opportunity to build a new life. There are about 71 million people in the world who have been forced to flee their homes. 26 million of these are official refugees living in another country. Another 41 million have fled their homes but remain in their country as internally displaced people (IDPs). More than 37,000 new people per day are forced to leave their homes.[14]

MEET A BIBLICAL REFUGEE

My grandfather immigrated to the land where I was born, which makes me a third-generation immigrant. I grew up in temporary housing and then had to flee to another country because my life was in danger. I was initially welcomed to this new country, but for twenty years my employer lied to me and continuously oppressed me. I finally returned to my homeland, but had to leave again because of a famine. I eventually ended my days in a foreign land, but my family will be able to bury me in the land of Israel. Once I summed up my life to a king by saying, "My life has been a pilgrimage, and my days on earth have been few and difficult" (Genesis 47:9). —JACOB, THE PATRIARCH

NEEDS OF REFUGEES

For a refugee, anywhere is better than their homeland. Their stories are tragic and traumatic because of war, persecution, or catastrophic natural disaster. Of all people on the move, refugees have the most needs and are also some of the most open to receive both physical and spiritual help. Regardless of your political position or how refugees came to your country, they are here and in great need. In fact, this may be the first time they have ever heard about Jesus since many come from places where following Jesus is a crime, churches do not exist and missionaries are forbidden entry. Many refugees' needs are basic: food, clothing, shelter, safety, access to healthcare and assistance with asylum process.

REFLECTING ON REFUGEES

02   Nearly every refugee has a difficult story of being forced to leave their home, family, culture. What would you take with you if you had to flee with only 15 minutes notice? Where would you go? After considering this, what other needs might a refugee have?

Open Your Eyes to See Professionals

People who migrate as professionals generally live in more developed countries due to their academic or career pursuits. Of the 66 million expats (people who live outside their native country) around the world, 46 million are skilled workers, and 5.5 million are international students.[15] This group is comprised of some of their home country's best and brightest. When they return to their home countries, they will likely be leaders in business, government, and social change. Professionals are usually educated, paid well, and tech savvy. Often professionals move with their families (who remain at home most of the time), travel frequently, and possess higher levels of influence.

MEET A BIBLICAL PROFESSIONAL

I am a man of great authority and great wealth. My curiosity took me to a foreign land over 1,300 miles away to learn about their festivals, their God, and read their holy writings. On my way back I was reading their holy writings, but not understanding what it was saying. Suddenly a man from that country met me and began talking with me. I was glad he was so bold, and I soon understood, believed, and was baptized in the name of his God. Now I will return to my country and can use my influence to lead others to the truth. —ETHIOPIAN TREASURER (ACTS 8:26-39)

NEEDS OF THE PROFESSIONALS

Professionals are those who *want* to be in your country and learn about your culture. The barriers to interaction are less because they know your language (or plan to learn it), yet still have relational needs that largely go unmet. Many work long hours and have little time for friends and fun. These people have a dream and are working to fulfill it. They generally enjoy new places, people, and cultures, but their success is what motivates them to live in your country. Food, hobbies, or things that help their success are good places to start building relationships with these people.

REFLECTING ON PROFESSIONALS

03   These foreigners usually have big dreams to fulfill, but are still far from their families, cultures, and everything familiar. Discuss what needs an international student or business person might have even though they *seem* to be adapting well to their new culture.

Open Your Eyes to See Near Neighbors

Minority ethnic groups who have been living in a country for a long time, even a generation or two, yet are still seen as "outsiders" may be referred to as near neighbors. They have maintained their ethnic identity and have learned how to live in both their home culture and their new culture. Migration is a part of the group's story, but not recently. They usually know several languages, work lower paying jobs, and only interact with the majority culture when they must (school, work, etc.). They rarely befriend someone from outside their home culture, but younger people do so more than older people. People from the majority culture rarely enter into their lives or culture, making them feel like outsiders forever. It is difficult to quantify this group, but it would be safe to say hundreds of millions fit into this category.

MEET A BIBLICAL NEAR NEIGHBOR

I know this will sound strange, but I was once possessed by many demons. They tormented me for years and had driven me to live alone and naked in the graveyard. The townspeople had tried to chain me, but I always broke free. Then one day, this Jewish rabbi drops anchor on my side of the lake. No Jews ever came to this side of the lake. He gets off the boat and walks right toward me. All of a sudden, something like lightning goes through me. I fell to the ground in pain, and the demons inside me started speaking to him. Again, another surge of pain as he tried to make them leave me alone. This man finally allowed them to go into some pigs and I found myself alone with him. He clothed me, comforted me, and told me to tell my village what God had done for me. I still wonder why he came to my side of the lake.

—GERASENE MAN (LUKE 8)

NEEDS OF NEAR NEIGHBORS

Living in two cultures with tension between them make friendships between the cultures rare. Near neighbors are proud of their culture yet also interested in their new culture (and many young people even more so). Their needs are more social and economic. Most want to advance beyond the status of their parents. Being bicultural, they can relate well to other bicultural people.

REFLECTING ON NEAR NEIGHBORS

04   Near neighbors operate in two worlds that are usually quite different. How might you feel as a minority person in your country needing to always go between two different cultures? What other needs might you have as a near neighbor?

🌱 Live

Make it Personal

01   Were you or your family ever a person in one of these categories? What was your experience like? How did you relate to the majority culture? What would have improved the experience?

<table>
<tr><td>Digging
Deeper</td><td>For more examples of the types of foreigners in the Bible, see
the Appendix: Lesson 3.</td></tr>
</table>

Make it Real

02   In the four categories of migrants, list the groups or individuals around you within each category. Try to list at least two people in each category. Then circle one of these people to visit this week over tea, coffee, or lunch. These people could be near or far, online or in person, someone you know well or someone you want to know. Ask God to open your eyes to see who is in your life.

Immigrants

Refugees

Professionals

Near Neighbors

Lesson 04

Obstacles *to* Welcoming

> But now in Christ Jesus you who once
> were far off have been brought near by
> the blood of Christ. For he himself is our
> peace, who has made us both one and has
> broken down in his flesh the dividing wall
> of hostility.
>
> —Ephesians 2:13-14

✳ Prep

01   Imagine inviting some new friends over for dinner. Would you make a plan? Would you serve something to eat and drink that would please your guests? Would you clean up your home before they arrived? Would you wear something nice? What would you do in your culture? Share a few ideas.

02   If you are like many people and cultures around the world, you might practice many of these. Hospitality to friends is common all over the world and is not something distinctly Christian (Luke 6:32-33). Now imagine having a family over from another culture you know very little about that is very different from your own. You probably have less in common with them. What thoughts would go through your head now? Share a few.

03   Now imagine inviting a person from a different culture over, but your people do not have good relations with them or maybe their people have harmed your people or family. What thoughts would go through your head now? Share a few.

04   Why are we most attracted to the first scenario, less to the second, and definitely not to the third?

We have looked at God's word and heart for the foreigner. We have considered the need and opportunity to welcome people worthy of our love and

compassion. We have ached with them and for them. Yet when God invites us into meaningful friendships with people from around the world so they might know him, it still seems so hard. Let's look at some of the reasons.

" Discuss

The Obstacle of Pride

Nobody wants to admit they are prideful, but it is unfortunately part of our sinful nature. Pride is the root of all kinds of evil in our world. We all usually default to loving ourselves, thinking of ourselves, taking care of ourselves, and standing up for what we deserve without thinking about what it will cost others. We ask, "What is in it for me?" We tend to avoid things that seem beneath us, make us insecure, do not seem worth our time, or do not give back to us. Why is this? Perhaps we have an excessive view of ourselves. Our souls may be restless and searching for worth, value, or meaning. Maybe we feel like we have something to prove or think that happiness lies in being better than others, doing more than others, or in being more successful than others. But as Christians we know that all we are and all we have comes from God (James 1:17, Romans 11:36). There is no place for pride—only humility and gratefulness.

PRIDE IN THE BIBLE

Possibly the most significant shift in the early church is recorded in Acts 10. Even though Peter knew Jesus had commanded his followers to go "make disciples of every nation" and "preach everywhere," he had refused to go to the Gentiles because of his pride. To Peter these foreigners were unclean. He and the whole Jewish church did not think the Gentiles were worthy or able to become followers of Jesus without becoming Jews first. But through a series of miraculous interventions by God, Peter renounced his pride and declared, "I now realize how true it is that God does not show favoritism, but accepts, from every nation, the one who fears him and does what is right" (Acts 10:34-35).

> **ⓘ Pride**
>
> a high view of oneself compared to others; conceit or ego

01   In the Bible, pride is something that God opposes. "All of you, clothe yourselves with humility toward one another, because 'God opposes the proud but shows favor to the humble'" (1 Peter 5:5). However, in today's culture, pride is often seen as a good quality. Why might pride stand as an obstacle to loving our neighbor? What examples of pride do you see in your culture or church toward people who are different?

02   Matthew 22:37-40 sums up the entire Bible in a sentence: "Jesus replied, 'Love the Lord your God with all your heart and with all your soul and with all your mind.' This is the first and greatest commandment. And the second is like it: 'Love your neighbor as yourself.' All the Law and the Prophets hang on these two commandments." What could it look like to love a particular foreigner or people group as much as you love yourself?

03   **Read Luke 9:51-56.**

How did Jesus' disciples display their pride when the Samaritans treated them unfairly? How did Jesus respond to them? What would have been a better response?

The Obstacle of Prejudice

Prejudice goes hand-in-hand with pride. Prejudice is when you prejudge someone with very little knowledge about them. We may have a little information about a person or culture (whether it is true or not) and then fill in the rest using information we have heard or assumptions we have made.

Psychologists tell us it is natural for humans to make distinctions between those like them and those different from them; they refer to these two groups as "us" and "them." The "us" is as fundamental as our family and friend group who we naturally trust and favor more. It also extends to those who have things in common with us: fans of our favorite sports team, our countrymen, those in our same economic position, or those of the same religion. By default, the "them" is everyone outside of those groups. We tend to exalt "us" and simultaneously look down upon "them."

For example, as new people come into our country, they initially need help with basic necessities like food, shelter, and medical care. Those in the host country can look at these true needs and assume the immigrant's goal is to continuously exploit the system, get free stuff, and never work for anything—all based on a story they heard from a friend or on TV. In reality, almost all immigrants desire to have a job, work hard, and earn their own way.

PREJUDICE IN MY CONTEXT

04   What examples of prejudice do you see in the culture of the church?

_____

_____

_____

_____

05   Those you are seeking to welcome also have pride in their culture and prejudices toward your culture. What might some of these be? What Christian attitudes or actions might help overcome their pride and prejudice?

_____

_____

_____

Digging Deeper

Jonah was a reluctant prophet sent by God to warn the Assyrians, the hated enemy of Israel, of God's coming wrath. Assyria had been oppressing Israel for years. Even modern historians comment that they were an exceptionally cruel people. God wanted to save the Assyrians, but Jonah's prejudice made him angry when they repented; he resented that God could be kind to Assyrians. How did God respond to Jonah's prejudice?

The Obstacle of Fear

FEAR OF BEING UNCOMFORTABLE

Welcoming involves stepping outside of our comfort zone and into someone else's world. You are going to a place you have never

 Fear

anxious concern caused by the perception of harm to yourself or others been to in order to talk with people you don't know who come from a different culture, who eat different food, and who might not speak your language. You might be asking yourself questions like these: *What will we talk about? Will they be able to speak my language? Do we have anything in common? What if I say something offensive? Will it be awkward?* Doing this is understandably scary and uncomfortable—as much for them as it is for you! As you press into what seem like unending differences, you will find how much you actually have in common and how their story and experience is similar to your own. You will see how inaccurate stereotypes can be and how the foreigner's deepest needs are the same as those of everyone else.

FEAR FOR MYSELF

Welcoming can involve the perception of danger—real or imagined. *What if they are opposed to my culture or government? If I talk about Jesus, will they hate me or become hostile?* Jesus never said following him was safe, but he did say he would always be with us and nothing could separate us from him.

FEAR OF FAILURE

What if I fail? I don't know what I'm doing! What if I do more damage than good? First, even the most seasoned missionary often feels this way. Second, most of the success in welcoming is just being present with people. Ninety percent of it is just showing up. Some Christians serve a lot, but never share Jesus; others preach a lot without meeting needs or showing basic love and dignity. Success in welcoming is both. It is being a witness for Jesus in both our words and our actions (Acts 1:8). Developing a genuine friendship is often the key to understanding the best way to meet their needs and to learn how to talk to them about Jesus. It is not your job to meet all of their needs or to "save" them. That is God's job. Love well, be a good friend, talk about each other's lives and share Jesus. God is very pleased with that.

> The remarkable thing about God is that when you fear God, you fear nothing else. —OSWALD CHAMBERS

When fear wins, we end up doing nothing because we are paralyzed by what we might lose. "There is no fear in love, but perfect love casts out fear" (1 John 4:18).

FEAR IN MY CONTEXT

06   What signs or examples of fear do you see in your culture or church toward outsiders?

07   Living in bondage to our fears is not living in the freedom Jesus calls us to. Read 2 Timothy 1:7, 2 Corinthians 12:9-10, and 1 John 4:18. How does the truth in these verses help us overcome our fears?

The Obstacle of Busyness

It takes time to develop meaningful relationships, especially with people from another culture. Our lives are full of activities. Most we choose. Some are chosen for us. Most people would like more room for family, friendships, exer-

cise, contributing positively to the world, etc., but feel like they cannot do these things because they are too busy. Being busy does not mean that we can opt out of obedience when God calls. And he has. We must prayerfully consider the opportunities surrounding us each day to "love our neighbor as [ourself]." Love is the greatest commandment (Mt. 22:38-40) and the highest virtue (1 Cor. 13:13) for the Christian. We make time for who or what we love.

 Busy

the state of having or being occupied by (too) many activities

BUSYNESS IN MY CONTEXT

08   What do you think causes us to be involved in so many activities? How can busyness can be an obstacle to welcoming our neighbor? What examples of busyness do you see in your culture or in the church?

> **"**
> If the devil cannot make us bad, he will make us busy.   — CORRIE TEN BOOM

09   Read James 4:13-17 and Galatians 6:9-10. How does God want us to view our time and the opportunities he brings each day? Name one way you can make more space in your life for relationships.

🌱 Live

Make it Personal

Sometimes the church takes on the prevalent political climate of the government or a society. If that is anti-immigrant, it can make welcoming outsiders difficult. Close personal friends may be passionately opposed to foreigners coming into the country. Many Christian people are fine with serving the marginalized but would be uncomfortable befriending them and would resist having them move into their neighborhood or become the majority at their church. We have looked at four major obstacles that exist in our lives, our churches, and our culture to welcoming people different from us. What other major obstacles might exist in your life or the church that we did not mention? What might be God's response to these?

Digging Deeper	Earlier we saw Peter's pride and how God changed him in Acts 10-11. Later in Peter's ministry we see him struggle with prejudice toward foreigners (Greeks) and fear of the religious establishment in Antioch. He even became an obstacle to other Christians looking to his leadership (i.e., Barnabas). In Galatians 2:11-14, what is Paul's response and why? What was at stake for him? What is at stake for the church today?

Make it Real

Change in the church begins one person at a time. It can begin with you. Ask yourself the honest question: Do I want to change in order to become a welcomer?

01   **Take a moment of silent prayer and read over this next part.**
     What is your biggest obstacle (pride, prejudice, fear, busyness, or other)? What examples can you think of? What is one way you commit to change?

Now take some time to share these (if you are in a group) and pray for one another, asking God for help.

Lesson 05

How Do I Welcome?

> " You shall treat the stranger who sojourns
> with you as the native among you, and
> you shall love him as yourself, for you were
> strangers in the land of Egypt: I am the Lord
> your God.
>
> —Leviticus 19:34

✳ Prep

Think back to the introduction to Lesson Four. We started out considering our response to having a friend, a stranger, and an enemy over for dinner. Hospitality to friends is common all over the world, but is not something distinctly Christian (Luke 6:32-33). But being a neighbor to those *not* like you, loving enemies, showing hospitality to strangers not from your "tribe" or nation... now that is distinctly Christian and takes the supernatural work of the Holy Spirit. It is a great start to just invite someone from another nation over, but do not stop there. We long to comfort them if they are in distress, be a friend if they are alone, and be God's invitation if they do not know him. But how do we do that? Welcoming is both natural and supernatural. In this lesson you will be given a model for welcoming. It recognizes the role you play and the role God plays.

What Welcomers Do: Pray, Care, Share

Welcomers are not spiritual superstars. They're people who simply love Jesus and want to follow him. They *pray* with and for foreigners. They *care* for them in practical ways by meeting their needs. They *share* who Jesus is and how he has changed their life.

❝ Discuss

Praying for the Foreigner

Think of people you know who would be considered outsiders by their majority culture. They could be from any of the groups of people we have talked about. These could be people you regularly see or just met. They could be coworkers, people who live near you, someone you share a common interest with (parenting, sports, politics, etc.), or someone that attends your school. You may know their name, you may not. God does. You may even start with people groups if you do not know a specific person yet.

01   Who are the outsiders in your community? Make a list of two to ten people (you may refer back to the people from previous lessons) for whom you want to start praying.

-------------------------   -------------------------   -------------------------

-------------------------   -------------------------   -------------------------

BEGIN TO PRAY WELCOMING PRAYERS

- Pray that God would move in their circumstances and their struggles.

- Pray for healing, belonging, a sense of dignity, and a home.

- Pray for their physical, emotional, and spiritual security.

- Pray for their children who understand so little of what is happening.

- Pray that God would reveal himself to them as the source of provision for all their needs.

- Pray for them to have visions and dreams of Jesus.

- Pray he would remove obstacles toward legal status, aid if needed, government services, viable employment, education, language, community, and integration within their new culture.

- Pray that God would bring them into your life and for you to have eyes to see when he does.

- Pray for your friendship.

- Pray that you would be a blessing to them.
- Pray 1 Kings 8:41-43 over them. Make a list of Bible passages and promises to pray for them.

02   Can you think of any other ways to pray for foreigners?

03   Write down a prayer for each person. Pray these to the Lord.

Pick a length of time to commit to pray for them daily. Two weeks might be a helpful starting place.

Caring for the Foreigner

Now that you have prayed for some people who have come from the ends of the earth" to your community, what is next? Ask yourself, "How can I be a blessing to them?" or "How can I enter their world and demonstrate Christ's love?" This is where caring comes in. Be a friend to them. You may have to think about some ways to cross cultures, but let Christ's love compel you, and you will find a way. Here are some ideas to get you started.

GO BE WITH THEM

It will likely be strange and difficult at first. Regardless of what barriers seem to exist—step out of your comfort zone and seek to demonstrate the practical love of Jesus by simply being with people. If there are organizations who already have structures for engaging with and serving foreigners, join them. In fact, flooding them with Christian volunteers will be a witness to both the organizations and the people they serve.

DISCOVER WAYS TO PRACTICALLY HELP THEM

As you learn about the foreigners in your community, you will also learn about their needs. When you engage in conversation with them, ask thoughtful questions and listen well. Inevitably this will lead to opportunities to care for them.

DEMONSTRATE HOSPITALITY

Food is always a good place to start. Invite them over for a meal or take one to them. You can explain to them what hospitality looks like in your culture and ask what hospitality looks like in theirs. Next time you host them, can you incorporate a welcoming tradition from their culture? It is common for them to offer to host you and introduce you to their family and friends.

BUILD GENUINE RELATIONSHIPS

Be genuinely interested in them, their family, and their situation. Feel free to prepare questions ahead of time so you can keep the conversation going. Ask them to teach you about their culture.

Invite them into your group of friends, and do intentional things to get to know each other. The gospel travels best across bridges of friendship. Just like your other friends, ask them to join you for some event you normally do. Perhaps it is watching TV, going to a movie, eating with friends, or playing games. The event is not as important as spending time with them and creating environments where you can have a conversation.

PRAY FOR THEM

Do not forget to ask if you can pray for them. Be sensitive and ask for permission to pray for them. It is a good idea to pray with them in the moment if possible.

IDEAS FOR CARING

These ideas may not work in every culture, but they can prompt you to discover other practical ways to interact cross-culturally within your specific context.

- Take them to a new market or grocery store
- Have coffee or tea
- Show them where the nearest parks are
- Invite them to a meal from your country or go to one from theirs
- Celebrate a holiday together
- Teach them to navigate the public transport system or drive in your area
- Take them to the doctor or other appointments
- Go exercise together
- Help them move if needed
- Help them learn the language or read mail they do not understand
- Help them with government bureaucracy
- Help their kids with homework or signing up for school/community activities
- Have a play date together with your children
- Learn ten basic words or phrases in their language

Digging Deeper	For more practical ideas on caring for foreigners, see the Appendix: Lesson 5.

Sharing with the Foreigner

04   **Read Acts 1:8, 1 Peter 3:15.**

What do these verses say about sharing Jesus with others?

ASK THEM ABOUT THEIR FAITH

Getting into spiritual conversations is key. Feel free to ask about their faith or what they believe and listen. Seek to understand and clarify what they mean. Do not correct or challenge, just show genuine interest in them as a person. As the Lord opens doors, they might ask you about what you believe. This is your invitation to share your beliefs.

MODEL YOUR GROWING RELATIONSHIP WITH JESUS

If they are spending time with you and your Christian friends, make it a habit to talk with each other about how Jesus is making a daily difference in your life. These spiritual conversations can easily lead into reading Bible stories about Jesus together. As you develop this skill, the Holy Spirit will help you connect everyday conversations to teachings of Jesus.

COMMON PITFALLS TO AVOID

01 **Don't try to share everything all at once.** There is rarely time to go from Genesis to Revelation in one conversation. This will also give you the opportunity to meet regularly as you continue the conversation.

02 **Don't try to defend institutional Christianity** or the actions of the church through the ages. Feel free to apologize for evil actions of the church or Christians and point out that Jesus would never have done them.

03 **Don't argue.** You are called to be a witness of Jesus. It is the Holy Spirit's job to convict and bring spiritual revelation.

04 **Don't feel like you have to have all the answers.** Be willing to admit what you don't know. If possible, look up answers later or be okay with knowing that some things are taken by faith. Christianity is a reasonable faith, but it still takes faith.

05 **Don't wait a long time in the relationship to begin these conversations.** It is okay to start in the first few interactions of the relationship. If you wait too long, they will think it is strange that you have never talked about Jesus before, though you claim he is so important to you. In fact, as you introduce yourself, it is often just as natural to talk about Jesus as it is to talk about your family. Many non-western cultures are very spiritual and often talk more openly about religion.

SAMPLE QUESTIONS

Here are some good questions to help you engage in spiritual conversations and share how they can belong to God's family:

01   Tell me about your spiritual journey. How did you become a _____?

02   I don't know too much about _____. Tell me more about how you came to believe this to be true?

03   What do you know about Jesus or his message? Have you ever personally known a follower of Jesus?

04   I like to pray for the people close to me. Is there a way I could specifically pray for you? Could I now? (Then ask about that issue later.)

05   May I share my story of how I began to follow Jesus?

06   Could I explain what it means to follow Jesus and you tell me what you think?

Digging Deeper	See the Appendix: Lesson 5 for a simple tool to outline the gospel called the Three Circles.

It should take a maximum of 15 minutes to share the first time. If they start following Jesus, teach the outline to them so they can share with others.

The goal is not merely to "share it" and be done, but rather to develop a genuine long-term friendship in which they see, hear, and experience the reality of God and the difference he makes in your life.

01   Would you ever be interested in reading some of Jesus' teachings with me? or I have a group that meets on _____ to study Jesus' teachings. Would you like to come?

02   Remember, it's the Holy Spirit who works through the Living Word to convict and change people's hearts.

Digging Deeper	See the Appendix: Lesson 5 for simple Discovery Bible Study principles and examples.

03   Which of these questions feel easy for you to use? Which ones feel hard? Why?

04   Do you know of any other questions that are helpful for starting spiritual conversations with others? Share a few with the group.

🌿 Live

Make it Real

From the list of two to ten people you wrote down in the "Pray" section, circle two people you feel especially called to pursue. Take a few minutes to write three questions for each person that might be helpful in starting spiritual conversations. Now pick one of your people and take turns role playing with a friend using your questions. Close by praying for each of you to be faithful to follow Jesus in whatever ways he wants to connect you to the foreigners in your community.

Developing *a* Welcomer Plan

" Let brotherly love continue. Do not neglect to show hospitality to strangers, for thereby some have entertained angels unawares.

—Hebrews 13:1-2

⚖ Plan

This training would not be complete without giving you a way to process all you have learned and obey what God is speaking to you. This may be the most important lesson.

Lets start with a group discussion and then give you some individual time to develop your plan.

> **ℹ Plan**
>
> an intention or decision

01 How does the group think your city or nation would change if Christians welcomed foreigners as this training described? Discuss this briefly.

_____

_____

_____

_____

Now take 10–15 minutes on your own to review your answers in the *Make it Real* sections in Lessons 1–5. They have been designed to help you craft your Welcomer Plan. Then answer the questions below.

02 What has the Lord been speaking to you throughout this study? Write down three ways God has spoken to you.

_____

_____

_____

_____

03 Read Matthew 7:24–27 and James 1:22–25. What do these verses say about hearing truth and not acting on it?

_____

_____

_____

_____

_____

_____

Take the Welcomer Pledge

Many people around the world have benefited from declaring their intention to be a Welcomer in some public way; we leave that up to you or your fellowship. You are invited to join the growing family of Welcomers around the world by making this pledge. If you have been convicted that you need to join the Lord in what he is doing among refugees, migrants, professionals, and/or near neighbors, then tell him and let someone else know. You may do this as a group or as an individual depending on your context and culture.

> By God's grace, I pledge to love the Lord and love my neighbors who are considered foreigners, whether they are immigrants, refugees, professionals, or near neighbors. I will follow Jesus' example and the Word of God to seek them out and bless them, even at a cost to myself. I will fail at times, but I will turn to the Lord when I do. If I can help raise up others to join me in welcoming the nations in my community, I will.

Name _____   Date _____

Finalizing Your Welcomer Plan

On the following pages, you will find several one-page Welcomer Plans. Identify one to three people you can welcome and take 15–30 minutes to fill out the Welcomer Plan(s) as completely as possible. Don't worry if you cannot answer every question. Some of the questions will be answered as you meet and get to know these people. Just keep adding information to your plan as your relationships progress. If you have no one, then start by making a plan to engage with a specific group and identify someone you can connect with. Reviewing Lesson 5 will help you find a place to start.

TIPS

- Remember that people are not projects. Please use this to build relationships with foreigners, not just fill out a form.

- Trust Jesus throughout this process, not plans and tools. Ask the Holy Spirit to give you wisdom and insight into their lives.

- Coordinate with others. If possible, develop your plan with others who are taking the Welcomer pledge. You will be able to craft a quality plan together, go welcome together, and support each other in this ministry.

- Share your plan. Once you complete your plan, share it with someone else and pray for each other. Sharing with your pastor is also a good idea.

- Pray over your plan. Take time to intercede for other Welcomers and for those you will be trying to welcome.

- You are committing to join God in his work of redeeming all nations. Because of your prayers and actions, lives are going to be changed for all of eternity. There are many obstacles in front of you, but we know Jesus has overcome them all (John 16:33).

Take it Further

As momentum for welcoming foreigners to your community grows, establishing a Welcomer Group might be the next step to growing a culture of welcoming. A Welcomer Group is made up of like-minded people who meet regularly to pray for, care for, and share with foreigners, as well as disciple other Welcomers. Think of it as a group of people who live out the mission of God in their community with a special emphasis on caring for those considered foreigners. See the Appendix under Lesson 6 for more details about starting a Welcomer Group.

Welcomer Plan

Person's name: _____

What I know about them:

_____

How I can **pray** for them:

_____

_____

I could bless, **care** for, or serve them by...

_____

_____

Spiritual conversations we have **shared**:

01

02

03

By what means will I seek to share the love and good news of Jesus? By when?

_____

_____

_____

Specific goals/requests I am trusting God for in this relationship:

_____

_____

How can I involve my family in welcoming others?

_____

_____

Who can join me or who can I bring with me so they see welcoming firsthand?

_____

Welcomer Plan

Person's name:

What I know about them:

How I can **pray** for them:

I could bless, **care** for, or serve them by...

Spiritual conversations we have **shared**:

01

02

03

By what means will I seek to share the love and good news of Jesus? By when?

Specific goals/requests I am trusting God for in this relationship:

How can I involve my family in welcoming others?

Who can join me or who can I bring with me so they see welcoming firsthand?

Welcomer Plan

Person's name:

What I know about them:

How I can **pray** for them:

I could bless, **care** for, or serve them by...

Spiritual conversations we have **shared**:

01

02

03

By what means will I seek to share the love and good news of Jesus? By when?

Specific goals/requests I am trusting God for in this relationship:

How can I involve my family in welcoming others?

Who can join me or who can I bring with me so they see welcoming firsthand?

Appendix & Resources

LESSON 1

Biblical Basis of Welcoming

These verses reveal how God views foreigners and expects his people to treat the foreigner. Besides these verses, the Bible also contains many examples of foreigners and their impact on the world around them.

OLD TESTAMENT

- Genesis 15:13
- Exodus 2:22
- Exodus 12:19
- Exodus 12:48–49
- Exodus 18:3
- Exodus 20:10
- Exodus 22:21
- Exodus 23:9
- Exodus 23:12
- Leviticus 16:29
- Leviticus 18:26
- Leviticus 19:9–10
- Leviticus 19:33–34
- Leviticus 20:2
- Leviticus 22:18
- Leviticus 23:22
- Leviticus 24:22
- Leviticus 25:6
- Leviticus 25:23
- Numbers 9:14
- Numbers 15:14–16

- Numbers 15:26
- Numbers 15:29
- Numbers 15:30
- Deuteronomy 1:16
- Deuteronomy 10:18–19
- Deuteronomy 14:29
- Deuteronomy 16:11
- Deuteronomy 23:7
- Deuteronomy 24:14–15
- Deuteronomy 24:17–18
- Deuteronomy 24:19–21
- Deuteronomy 26:5
- Deuteronomy 26:11
- Deuteronomy 26:12–13
- Deuteronomy 27:19
- Deuteronomy 28:43
- Deuteronomy 31:12
- Joshua 8:35
- Joshua 20:9
- Ruth 2:10
- 1 Kings 8:41–43

- 1 Chronicles 22:2
- 1 Chronicles 29:15
- 2 Chronicles 2:17
- 2 Chronicles 6:32–33
- 2 Chronicles 30:25
- Job 31:32
- Psalm 39:12
- Psalm 94:6
- Psalm 105:12, 23
- Psalm 119:19
- Psalm 146:9
- Isaiah 14:1
- Jeremiah 7:6
- Jeremiah 22:3
- Ezekiel 14:7
- Ezekiel 22:7
- Ezekiel 22:29
- Ezekiel 47:22–23
- Zechariah 7:10
- Malachi 3:5

EXAMPLES OF ISRAEL WELCOMING WELL

- Rahab risked her life to welcome foreigners (Israelite spies). She was then welcomed in return by Israel. As both a foreigner and a Welcomer, "Rahab the foreigner" became a direct ancestor of Jesus (Matthew 1:5) and is commended for her great faith (Hebrews 11:31).

- Ruth welcomed and then took care of Naomi when she was a foreigner in Moab. The Israelite community then welcomed Ruth well as they extended the rights for foreigners to glean the edges of their fields. In the process she married Boaz, and "Ruth the foreigner" (book of Ruth) became the great-grandmother of King David and a direct ancestor of Jesus (Matthew 1:5).

- When Solomon dedicated the Lord's temple he specifically prayed about foreigners and his desire for them to come to God. This bold prayer was answered in profound ways when the Queen of Sheba and many kings came from distant lands to hear the wisdom God had put in Solomon's heart (2 Chronicles 9, 1 Kings 4 & 10). Solomon welcomed them well resulting in all glorifying the one true God.

- Both Isaiah (Isaiah 56:6–7) and Jesus (Mark 11:17) spoke about this theme of the temple being a place for foreigners to come and pray and be welcomed to meet with God.

- The Samaritan took practical action (Luke 10:25–37):

  - He took time to notice the man
  - He was filled with compassion for him and his situation
  - He looked beyond culture, ethnicity, and centuries of ethnic conflict and chose to help
  - He risked his own wellbeing
  - He used his own resources to save the man
  - He personally cared for him
  - He empowered others to care for him

NEW TESTAMENT: JESUS' LIFE AND MINISTRY

- Matthew 1:5
- Matthew 2:1–12
- Matthew 4:24–25, Mark 3:7–8, Luke 6:17
- Matthew 8:5–13, Luke 7:1–10
- Matthew 8:28–34, Mark 5:1–20, Luke 8:26–39
- Matthew 11:21–22, Luke 10:13–14
- Matthew 11:23–24, Luke 10:15
- Matthew 12:41, Luke 11:32
- Matthew 12:42, Luke 11:31
- Matthew 15:21–28, Mark 7:24–30
- Matthew 15:29–39, Mark 7:36–37
- Matthew 25:35,38
- Mark 7:31–35
- Mark 9:33–37
- Mark 11:17, Isaiah 56:6–8
- Luke 4:24–30
- Luke 10:25–37
- Luke 17:11–19
- John 4:5–52
- John 12:17–33

NEW TESTAMENT: EXPANSION OF THE GOSPEL BY FOREIGNERS IN ACTS

- **Acts 8:5–39**
  Philip & the Ethiopian eunuch

- **Acts 11:19–26**
  Persecuted believers & the church in
  Antioch

- **Acts 28:11–16**
  Paul in Rome

LESSON 3

Four Categories of Foreigners in the Bible

REFUGEE

- Abraham & Sarah
- Isaac & Rebekah
- Joseph
- Jacob & family
- Moses
- David

- Slave girl of Naaman
- Nation of Judah
- Shadrach, Meshach, & Abednego
- Daniel
- Ezekiel

- Jewish diaspora 1st Century BC
- Joseph, Mary, Jesus
- Early church (from Jerusalem)

IMMIGRANT

- Abraham & Sarah
- Rebekah
- Joshua

- Israelites out of Egypt (Exodus)
- Rahab
- Naomi

- Ruth
- Jonah
- Paul

PROFESSIONAL

- Queen of Sheba
- Regional kings near Solomon

- Naaman
- Cornelius, family & friends

- Ethiopian eunuch
- Lydia

NEAR NEIGHBOR

- Widow of Zarephath
- Syrian army
- Samaritan leper
- Crowds (1000s who came to Jesus)
- Roman centurion
- Syrophoenician women

- Greek visitors
- Samaritan women
- Gerasene demoniac
- Deaf man
- Crowd of 4000 men, plus women and children

LESSON 5

Care

Here are some more ideas on welcoming people from around the world that might spark an idea for you:

01 If possible, check the county register to welcome every new person to your area in the last few months. Bring them a welcome note, food, and offer to help them learn their new city. Many foreigners struggle to make friends and find their way in a new country.

02 Eat at cross-cultural restaurants and get to know foreigners. They have some delicious food!

03 Befriend an imam or another religious leader and genuinely ask good questions, listen, and serve them. You will be surprised at how friendly they are.

04 Learn about different religions, especially the ones closest to you. We live in a such a multi-religious world now. It shows respect, raises your cultural IQ, and helps you interact with someone from that religion.

05 Host a Welcoming the Nations group in your church or town. Bringing others along in your adventure will make it more impactful and longer lasting.

06 Start or serve with a ministry that crosses cultural, tribal, or language lines in your city.

07 Find a way to bless a local migrant people. Find out who is in charge (if someone *is* in charge) and ask what needs the migrants might have. Most times physical needs are met first. Start a clothes or food collection from local churches, a lay language school, or another activity that gets you interacting with and blessing them.

08 Research who is in your village or city from another nation or people group. This could help many churches in your area to be more strategic in welcoming or serving them. Most churches just don't know. One good online tool for North America is peoplegroups.info. You can search for a people group or see who is in your city.

LESSON 5
Share — The Three Circles[16]

This diagram gives an overview of the whole Bible focusing on how we can come back to God as our King and return from brokenness to God's true design. Share the illustration on a paper or napkin (or whiteboard for a large group) and answer any questions people may have.

CIRCLE 1: BROKENNESS

(Draw and label circle 1) This is the story that is changing the lives of people all over this world. As you look at the world, you do not have to look far to see suffering, oppression, corruption, war, famine, environmental disasters, broken families, and broken people everywhere. Our world is broken. **Read John 10:10.** Everyone is trying to find a way out through **(draw arrows)** things like education, money, religion, drugs, politics, etc., but these things do not take away sin or our brokenness. However, God did not create the world like this.

CIRCLE 2: GOD'S PERFECT DESIGN

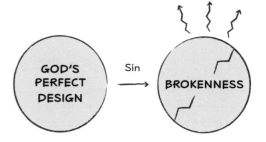

(Draw and label circle 2) God created a good world free from all this suffering. His design was a place where people were rightly related to him, others, themselves, and the earth. But through sin, **(draw arrow and "Sin")** humanity departs from God's perfect design and brokenness entered our lives, our families, our cultures, and our institutions. **Read Romans 3:23 and 6:23.** However, God did not leave us there.

CIRCLE 3: JESUS

(Draw and label circle 3) Jesus provides a way to come out of brokenness, be forgiven, and be rightly related to God again. He did this by living a perfect life, and then choosing to go to the cross, **(draw cross)** where he took our shame, guilt, and brokenness. He rose again, conquering sin and death and now offers forgiveness and restoration to us as a gift through faith. **Read John 3:16 or 14:6.** He calls us turn from our way, **(draw arrow and "Turn & surrender")** and surrender our life to him as our Lord **(draw crown). Read Ephesians 2:8–9, Romans 10:9, 2 Corinthians 5:21, or 1 Peter 3:18.**

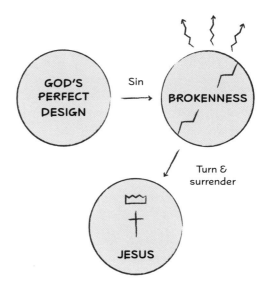

CONNECTING THE CYCLE

But God's desire is not just our forgiveness. He wants us to follow him into this new life by obeying his Word **(draw arrow and "Follow")** and that we would help others out of their brokenness **(draw arrow and "Fish"). Read Mark 1:17.**

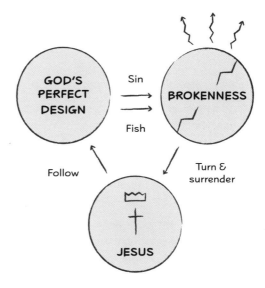

KEY QUESTIONS

01. Where are you in the drawing (Brokenness or God's Design)?

02. Where would you like to be?

03. Where are your friends?

Let them answer each question before asking the next. If they want to follow Jesus, ask them the 3rd question; if they do not, then the first two questions are sufficient.

If you wish to see a presentation by a 10-year-old (you can do this!), check out https://youtu.be/ZF75A3WX7FQ. There are many more examples out there. The point is to learn a strategy that you are comfortable with and can explain anywhere in any amount of time.

LESSON 5

Share — Discovery Bible Study[17]

The primary purpose of a Discovery Bible Study (DBS) is to lead readers into a knowledge and understanding of Scripture that moves them towards practical application (2 Timothy 3:15–17). The DBS method allows a group to study Scripture in a way that levels the playing field; no one is the expert. Whether a seasoned believer or hearing a Bible story for the first time, no one can bring outside knowledge or information; all conclusions are drawn from the specific passage read at the time, nothing more and nothing less. All-in-all, a DBS is not just Scripture-based, but also Scripture-only.

As new scriptures are introduced, the group learns a vital principle of interpretation: scripture interprets scripture. Without fail, they adjust and grow in their understanding of Scripture at a deeper level than a student-teacher approach would because it is the Holy Spirit speaking through the word to each individual.

So how does this practically play out? Below is an example. Mary (in the example below) is more familiar with the student-teacher approach and joins a DBS. See why DBS avoids this approach in favor of scripture interpreting scripture.

> **Facilitator:** What is this passage in Genesis 1 saying?
>
> **John (unbeliever):** It says to me that God made everything (scriptural conclusion).
>
> **James (new believer):** This passage tells me that God made everything around me. If that is true, then we have a responsibility to look after it. This week, I will make a point of picking up litter and looking after the world that God created (scriptural conclusion and obedience statement).
>
> **John:** It seems to be saying that God made everything in six days and then rested on the seventh day. I have been working a lot lately, but if God saw the need to take time to rest, then I also need rest. I will take time this week to rest and spend time with my family (scriptural conclusion and obedience statement).
>
> **Mary (believer):** Well, I don't believe God made the world in six literal days. If you allow me, then I can show you that the days were not literal, but figurative. Also, Jesus did away with the Sabbath. In Hebrews, it says... (approaching Scripture with a doctrinal premise and using Scripture to try to prove a point).
>
> **Facilitator:** Which part of the text sparked that idea?
>
> **Mary:** Well, I just read a commentary once that got me thinking...

Facilitator: Thanks for that idea, Mary, but hold that thought. For our purposes here, just stick to the Bible for this time.

Mary (gets offended): Well, if you don't want to hear what I have to say, then fine. I think it is important for these new believers to understand what the Bible really says! They can easily fall into error, you know!

What is taking place in this interaction? The unbeliever and new believer deal with the passage before them and instinctively follow the process of "simple truth simply obeyed." Mary enters the discussion with a set of preconceptions and muddies the understanding and application of the passage.

Mary's student-teacher approach can hinder replication. The new believer may think that they need an "expert" to lead a DBS and, as a result, may never invite friends to study the Bible with them. However, when followed, the DBS approach keeps the Word of God as the central authority. This is easily replicated. The group does not need a Bible expert to lead the group — they simply need a Bible. Members of the group quickly understand this and develop a boldness to start groups of their own.

RULES FOR A DBS:

01 When retelling the story, stick to what is in the passage. Don't add or change the passage or include interpretation in your telling.

02 No individual may impose their "insight" on others — stick with the plain and simplest meaning of the passage in front of the group. (No talk about sermons or commentaries.)

03 Any individual may challenge any other individual in the group with one simple question: "Where does it say what you are saying in this passage of Scripture?"

DBS STEPS:

01 Select someone to read the passage.

02 Have someone else read the same passage a second time.

03 Ask someone who did not read the passage to retell the story in their own words without looking at the passage.

04 After they are done, have the group correct either what was left out or added to the story using Scripture.

05 Repeat steps 3 and 4 with someone else retelling the story in their own words.

3 Simple Questions:

- What does this story teach us about God?
- What does this story teach us about people?
- How can we apply these stories to our lives?

These steps may seem like a lot to follow, but it is simple once you go through it! Just remember to have the passage read and retold twice and then open up discussion with the three questions about God, people, and personal application.

TIPS FOR THE FACILITATOR:

01   Remind the group of the rules and encourage all members to contribute.

02   It may be necessary to help people find their way around the Bible and to explain the meaning of some words at the start of the study. The facilitator is to avoid telling or drawing on other sources of information, but should ask questions or point to verses which may hold clues. If teaching is required, this is best provided in bite-sized pieces to allow digestion and interaction.

03   Don't be worried by silence. Seekers and new believers are often reading to get a sense of the story. Don't fill stretches of silence with your answers.

04   Call people back when getting off track by saying "Which part of the text sparked that idea?" or "Thanks for that idea, but can we hold that thought as we need to stick to the Bible for this time."

SUGGESTED PASSAGES FOR A DBS:

- **Genesis 1:1–25**
  The Creation Story: God Creates the World

- **Genesis 2:4–24**
  The Creation Story: The Creation of Man

- **Genesis 3:1–13**
  The Fall: The First Sin and Judgment

- **Genesis 3:14–24**
  The Fall: Judgment of a Sinful World

- **Genesis 6:1–9:17**
  The Fall: The Flood

- **Genesis 12:1–8, 15:1–6**
  Redemption: God's Promise to Abram

- **Genesis 22:1–19**
  Redemption: Abraham offers Isaac as a Sacrifice

- **Exodus 12:1–28**
  Redemption: The Promise of Passover

- **Exodus 20:1–21**
  Redemption: The Ten Commandments

- **Leviticus 4:1–35**
  Redemption: The Sacrificial System

- **Isaiah 53**
  Redemption: Isaiah Foreshadows the Coming Promise

- **Luke 1:26–38, 2:1–20**
  Redemption: The Birth of Jesus

- **Matthew 3; John 1:29–34**
  Redemption: Jesus is Baptized

- **Matthew 4:1–11**
  Redemption: The Temptation of Christ

- **John 3:1–21**
  Redemption: Jesus and Nicodemus

- **John 4:1–26, 39–42**
  Redemption: Jesus and the Woman at the Well

- **Luke 5:17–26**
  Redemption: Jesus Forgives and Heals

- **Mark 4:35–41**
  Redemption: Jesus Calms the Storm

- **Mark 5:1–20**
  Redemption: Jesus Casts Out Evil Spirits

- **John 11:1–44**
  Redemption: Jesus Raises Lazarus from the Dead

- **Matthew 26:26–30**
  Redemption: The First Lord's Supper

- **John 18:1–19:16**
  Redemption: Jesus is Betrayed and Condemned

- **Luke 23:32–56**
  Redemption: Jesus is Crucified

- **Luke 24:1–35**
  Redemption: Jesus Conquers Death

- **Luke 24:36–53**
  Redemption: Jesus Appears and Ascends

- **John 3:1–21**
  Redemption: We Have a Choice

LESSON 6
Welcomer Groups

A Welcomer Group is like-minded people, who preferably have gone through this training, who will meet regularly to pray for, care for, and share with foreigners as well as find and train new welcomers. It is a group of people who live out the mission of God in community with a special emphasis on those considered foreigners.

SUGGESTED CORE VALUES

01   Be a lifelong learner about our missionary God (Rom. 12:2, 3 John 4–6).

02   Take personal responsibility to love your neighbor as yourself through welcoming those considered foreigners.

03   Focus on actually doing personal ministry to foreigners, not just talking about it (Mt. 28:19–20, Rom. 12:4–8).

04   Be a welcomer with others who want to do the same (even beyond your local fellowship). From the community comes godly accountability, regular meetings, challenge, mutual learning, and encouragement. Our unity honors God, is a witness to others, and strengthens the Body of Christ (John 17:21–23, Eph. 4:1–16).

05   Join God and the growing global movement of believers who are seeking to introduce those least reached by the gospel (Rom. 15:20–21). Many of the those considered foreigners come from places with little access to the gospel. God has brought a "foreign mission field from the ends of the earth" to your community. What an opportunity! See the rest of *Explore the World Christian Lifestyle* as a resource to help you understand more about the unreached and the mission of God.

SUGGESTED CORE PRACTICES FOR EVERY MEETING

01   **Commitment to Community**
Meet together weekly at a regular time.

02   **Commitment to Godly Stewardship**
Contribute financially, investing in ministries that serve the stranger, outsider, or the foreigner — especially those coming from least-reached peoples.

03   **Commitment to Intercessory Prayer**

Pray using ideas from the "Pray" section of Lesson 5 or other prayer resources.

04 **Commitment to Welcome**

Welcome someone in some way each week by caring or sharing. Make sure to share those stories of encouragement with group.

STEPS FOR STARTING A WELCOMER GROUP

01 Who can you think of who might join your group from your community? You will need at least two others to start. Look in other places for mission-minded Christians in your community and share the vision with them.

02 At your first gathering, talk about what you have learned and how that has impacted your life. See if they will go through Welcoming the Nations. Upon completion, ask them to sign the pledge and join you. It is good to invite them along and let them observe you welcoming others.

03 Practice the Core Practices each week. (If you wish to go beyond welcoming, see *Explore the World Christian Lifestyle* for more ideas of other ways to participate in God's mission and incorporate one or two over time.)

Endnotes

1   *Future of the Global Church*, by Patrick Johnstone, IVP p.143, 2011

2   United Nations. DESA / Population Division. 2019 Revision of World Population Prospects. Retrieved from population.un.org/wpp

3   Our World in Data. (2018) Retrieved from ourworldindata.org/urbanization

4   United Nations. (2018) Retrieved from un.org/development/desa/ publications/2018-revision-of-world-urbanization-prospects.html

5   Johnstone, p.7

6   Jesus Film Project. (2019) Retrieved from jesusfilm.org/strategies-and-tools/strategies/project-detail-translating.html

7   Johnstone, p.7

8   Open Doors. (2019) Retrieved from opendoorsusa.org/christian-persecution/stories/christian-persecution-by-the-numbers

9   International Labor Office. (2017) Retrieved from ilo.org/wcmsp5/ groups/public/@dgreports/@dcomm/documents/publication/ wcms_575479.pdf

10   Johnstone, p.7

11   Ibid.

12   Ethnologue. (2019) Retrieved from ethnologue.com/guides/ethnologue200

13   Equality Now. (2019) "The Equality Approach to Addressing Sex Trafficking." Retrieved from d3n8a8pro7vhmx.cloudfront.net/ equalitynow/pages/266/attachments/original/1527182554/Equality_Now_ Sex_Trafficking_Fact_Sheet.pdf?1527182554

14   UNHRC. (2018) Retrieved from http://www.unhcr.org/globaltrends2018.

15   Finacord. (2019) "Global Expatriates: Size, Segmentation and Forecast for the Worldwide Market." Retrieved from finaccord.com/ getattachment/Home/About-Us/Press-Releases/Global-Expatriates-Size,-Segmentation-and-Forecas/press_release_global_expatriates_size_ segmentation_forecast_worldwide_market.pdf.aspx?lang=en-US

16   Adapted from *T4T* by Steve Smith and Ying Kai

17   Adapted from *No Place Left* and Parkway Fellowship International Prayer Center

Notes

Notes